Deeply Infinitely Completely

Deeply Infinitely

Completely

By: Sebastian Alvarez

with Valeria Lopez

DEEPLY INFINITELY COMPLETELY

Copyright © 2021 by Sebastian Alvarez and Valeria

Lopez

All rights reserved. This book may not be reproduced

or used in any manner in whole or in part without written

permission from the author, except by a reviewer who may

quote brief passages in a review; nor may any part of this

book be reproduced, stored in a retrieval system, or

transmitted in any form or by any means including

photocopying, recording, or other electronic or mechanical

methods without written permission from the author.

ISBN: 9798595763349

I dedicate this book to you. You, who are too humble to see

your great talents. Surely after this, you will realize that I was

never lying about how incredibly talented and amazing you

are. Now the world will see you for the great talent and

biggest heart that you have. I love you.

- Valeria

In publishing this book, I am sharing with our readers, our most intimate and deepest moments. His words began as only beautiful works of art for my eyes. As time passed I realized that his words, our words, were meant to touch the eyes, heart, and lives of many more. This is our love story.

Heaven and Earth

What is love, but the inexplicable absence of breathable air
when gazing at the one.

To feel liberated, to be loved, and to possess an
unquenchable thirst for their presence.

If hands, feet, eyes, ears, arms and legs, all have pairs why
shouldn't hearts?

Mine is with yours, just as yours is with mine,

Does anything else matter?

If we are all but doomed to die alone, then I'll have died with
your name on my lips.

And your love permanently etched on my very soul, like a
distinguishable mark

Whose only worthy audience are the stars above.

Why is it that the way we love one another is riddled with
complexity?

We spend all of our time pretending we know the first thing
about love.

Deceiving ourselves into painting a picture of it in our head.

Until we meet someone like you.

With just one look and one word

Everything comes crashing down, and the fall is a swift one.

I don't mind because I know you'll be there to catch me.

Even with that risk, the odds with you are well worth it.

Beauty unmatched with any but nature.

To lay eyes upon you and heaven would be one and the same

Is there a difference to me?

Not at all.

Found

If it is really true

That God gives us two of everything except two hearts,

Then I know you have the one that goes with mine.

In a sky full of thousands of stars

You're the one that shines the brightest to me.

La estrella de mi vida.

I swear you grow more beautiful every day.

Maybe it's the love,

This love that grows inside of me.

From my heart, for your heart.

From me to you.

In a world full of captivating sights

You are the one that holds my gaze the longest.

The Stars, The Moon, The Ocean, The Sun.

None.

None so beautiful than the one I call mine.

The little piece of heaven I've been blessed with.

My little piece of heaven; my paradise.

The deep blue's icy depths don't do the depths of my love
justice.

Neither does the distance from the moon and back.

My love, from me to you, my yearning ever – beating heart waiting for yours.

The other half once searched for …

Finally found.

Sin

In this world of hate and greed,

Your love is like a shining beacon of hope that keeps me
going.

Your love heals my soul and invigorates my body.

Revitalizes my heart and grants me peace of mind.

If everything slowly kills you and loving you is a sin

Then let me be the martyr and sinner.

10 months

For 10 months I've had the opportunity to share memories, love, and be with the most amazing woman. Baby you've given me more than I could have hoped for and you've made me a very happy man. My interest for you became liking … infatuation, it became love and it's evolved and grown every single day; so much so that I can't live without you. Your smile is my light of day and your laugh is the very air I need to breathe. Your love is the fuel that makes my heart beat and baby I can't seem to get enough of you. I want to be with you, not only for 10 months … but for 20, 30, 40, babe numbers don't mean a thing to me as long as your heart is mine.

Happy 19 Months My Queen

I can't believe I've spent more than a year and a half with you. I am so blessed, so lucky, and so happy that only I have the luxury of calling you mine. I've told you a thousand times how I feel about you, but on this special day I want to remind you of how crazy in love I am with you. Babe you are the light that brightens my world, giving it meaning and purpose. I have never wanted to protect so precious of a life as yours. I honestly don't know what I'd do or who I'd be without you, because you make me strive to be a better man. A better man for you and for the family I very much would like to have with you. I have never been more serious about building a family with you, I want to share my life with you, make you my wife, the mother of my children. It's crazy how when I first met you, I was captivated by you, attracted to you like a bee to the sweet scent of honey. You were and are everything I want and ever need, the true definition of a woman. Loyal, loving, caring, and intelligent, an exquisite beauty that takes my breath away. I had the strong urge to know more about you, really know you. Almost like god was telling me already that you would be a huge part of my life. The more I got to know you, the more I realized how perfect you were for me and how much love I'd grown to hold for you. I would die for you, but living with you would be so much sweeter. Because every laugh I hear from you, every smile I see on your soft and luscious lips, every glance you take my way with those deep hazel, warm eyes; makes me fall for you more and more. Loving you was the easiest thing in the world for me, my heart never stood a chance, I just fell and fell. Even now I keep falling for you, amazed at how deep love can be and what the right person can do to your life. My Queen, My World, The Love of My Life… My Future Wife, thank you for doing everything you do for me and for standing next to me through all these months. If saving one person makes a difference in the world, then you have made all the difference in mine.

Sound of Beauty

My beauty, my sweet.

You play such a lovely tune, unheard to all but one.

The sound of beauty to me is in your smile, that warm hug you give.

Those big hazel eyes play a tune of longing, deep within, my heart stirs, awakened by the sweet sound of your beauty.

Silently an orchestra plays a timid but powerful rhythm with your three words, on and on it plays.

I am blissful.

I am whole.

You my love, play the sound of passion and devotion.

You intoxicate my every sense, leave me breathless, listening, yearning for more sounds.

The sounds of your beauty …

The only sound I hear from you.

Like my favorite song, playing on and on, endlessly for eternity.

For how can beauty sound, if not of the heart?

For flesh plays loud in youth, but soft with age.

But you, my beauty, my sweet.

Your heart plays now and forever.

To me, my darling, my love

You are the sound of beauty.

Babe…Happy 9 Months! I can't express how much I love

you but I will try with this poem I thought of…

Eternal

If there existed an eternal Garden of Eden, whose flowers
never withered or died…

Whose radiance never faltered or dimmed…

And if this garden grew the most exquisite flowers, blooming
orchids, purple lilacs, tulips and daisies of every color

And if in this garden resided a rose bush of exceptional
beauty…

I would take the time to search for the fairest, most vibrant
rose I could possibly find, and pluck it from its eternal resting
place

And I am so sure this flowers' radiance would never falter
and it would never wither and die…

For this flower would represent the absolute love and
devotion I have for you.

And this flower would be all that is good, all that is pure.

For my love for you is like this flower.

Never faltering, never fading, and never dying.

Good morning My Queen… I know you must feel drained and dim of your light so that's why I have to say…

You are truly a creature of the universe that possesses infinite beauty. Not because your beautiful soul is reflected in your physical vessel. I talk of the beauty I see in you… watching you touch everything around you and leaving it better than it was before. The beauty in how you treat everyone around you with love and a gentleness only the softest touch possesses. Cast away the costume you wear of doubt, sadness and uncertainty. You hold a unique universe inside you that we ALL need to see. Cast light on this world and vanquish the shadows by wearing your true essence, your true self. By being you and doing what your heart tells you to do. I know you are living as the best possible YOU, you can be/achieve.

I love you and I want to see that beauty that shines so bright… even if your light is too bright, I won't EVER look away.

2 Years

It's been two years since the day I made one of the best choices in my life. That means that for 24 months/104 weeks/73 days/17,520 hours/1,051,200 minutes/63,072,000 seconds you have dominated my heart and the better part of my mind. But you know what? Time is irrelevant when our love is forever. I will never stop loving you. Not in life or death, not with 10 years or 100,000,000,000,000,000,000,000,000,000,000,000,000,000,000,000 years. Time means nothing to me when I know the meaning of infinite. You are ∞ and the bridge that connects my soul to this world. Without you as my anchor, I would surely drift into oblivion. The world is a hard place to live in. One must find those moments of peace and tranquility in the chaos of reality. Babe you are that peace in my struggle. To say you are an oasis in a desert devoid of life does not do you justice. On the days I must be like Atlas, whom has the weight of the world crushing his shoulders, you make me feel like I am floating through the rivers of Eden. For that must be what Heaven feels like. What else would rejuvenate and restore your weary, bruised body. On days where stepping forward feels like it crushes my bones to dust and powder, you strengthen my soul. My love… you have brought heaven on earth to me, I belong to you, as you belong to me. My Queen, I am nothing without you by my side. And I am nobody without you in my life.

Happy Anniversary.

Thank you for 2 years.

Worthwhile

Where we go after death I do not know.

But if it is a bad place I want to make the most out of my life here on earth.

And if it's a good place I want to be worthy of living in it…

Never Stopped

To be honest with you, I never stopped.

I never stopped loving you.

Never stopped caring for you.

The switch never turned off, it stayed on.

On and on and on.

Every day it's a battle.

A battle that I will surely lose.

7 Months

Happy 7 months babe!

God I love you so much it hurts. You've been an amazing girlfriend and an even better woman in my life. I'm so blessed to call you mine, my cuddle bug/boo bear. My heart belongs only to you.

Te amo con todo mi corazon

Je t'aime de tout mon cuore

Ti amo con tutto il cuore

The language is different but the message is the same, I really do love you with all my heart and I could say it in a hundred languages and still wouldn't be able to fully explain just how strongly I feel for you!

Here's to 7 months:

7 reasons why I love you…

1. I love your laugh, it's music to my ears

2. Your smile lights up my world

3. I love when you turn red, it's super cute

4. I love your kind and caring heart

5. I love the way you look at me

6. I love that you can and DO cook amazing food/desserts for me

7. The 7th reason is probably the most important… because the previous reasons and so much more, I can't even begin to describe them all; all these things make me fall in love with you every day more and more

I am Sorry

If we are given two sets of keys at birth,

One set to open the gates of Heaven,

And the other set to open Hell

I have thus far chosen the latter.

So much doubt and uncertainty.

I wonder what happened

To the man who would wait a year

For your loving embrace and caress

So much pain and tears…

My own hand is to blame.

But I won't give up.

For as long as you'll have me

I will fight this darkness residing within

I am sorry it has taken this long

For any awareness of my faults to manifest itself.

The Automatic Meeting

There I was, sitting in class

And there She was, quiet, serene

Captivated I was by her silent beauty

As if by fate my body knew…

I knew there was a reason for this…

This state of entrancement I fell victim to.

Your magical aura won me before even I knew.

I was yours before I had even said hello.

Now dear I've seen the stars…

But your eyes are a wonder unknown…

For although I have the honor…

The deep honor of holding their infinite gaze,

I doubt I will ever solve the mystery.

The mystery of how her eyes had me before I had even said
"hello."

Illuminating Vulnerability

Like the gentle spring breeze

Ruffling my un kept hair

Your hands delicately soothe

The agitation within my soul.

This feeling that swells

Inside my chest, a byproduct

Of my love for you.

Take my heart and do what you will

Be it pain, pleasure, joy or sorrow

In the end, all is worth it.

For this vulnerability brought

About by this newfound love,

Brings clarity and purification.

Shattered Walls

Was it by the first look or the hundredth?

Your life force so strong it might as well have been the first look I got of you that stole my heart.

How could I ever know the love of my life would share my fate so early on in life?

How could I know that the very first smile I got from you on that bench would be the last time my heart opened for someone?

Why?

Because even now the last person to open up my heart to is and always will be…

You.

Even in Tough Times

Stalwart is my faith in you and us.

This bond between you and I?

Unbreakable, unforgettable.

Understand that through all the ups and downs, arguments,
and fights

I will always be here.

Even if miles and distance move to separate…

This place you hold in my heart is like no other.

Irreplaceable, unforgettable,

Like the feeling of the mornings first stretch.

Pure bliss is our time together,

Absolute agony when the time is up.

Light of my heart… keep shining,

And never change.

What I WILL Say

High school so bittersweet.

I hated it

But loved you.

Now I am at a crossroads.

When people ask me about high school what shall I say?

That the classes were boring and long?

That the homework was hard and stressful?

Will I complain about losing all my friends and connections?

I don't think so.

What I will say with a great big smile!

Is that I'd go through it all over 100x

Because high school…

Is where I met you.

Everlasting Moment

Never will I forget the joy

Of experiencing your presence

For the first time.

Calm captivating gaze,

Sparking warmth within.

Reigniting the faltering flame,

Of my belief in Love.

Like a revelation in crisis,

Or a fresh breath of air

The clarity you conceive…

My mind wakes from

Restless slumber.

My eyes fall on you and..

My heart falls for you.

Truth Revealing Darkness

If the moon is destined by fate to appear at the darkest hour;

My relieved face reveals the truth of the matter.

"You are my moon," quite simply,

The words cascading down my lips and onto fresh air.

The moon whose bright rays push back against any doubt or fear.

My Moon, you illuminate my darkness.

Guide me towards a brighter future,

A new day, new hope.

Home

Morning dew glistening droplets…

Either condensing or falling slow and steady.

The creaking porch, cool against the warm sun...

As it rises against the night, the light permeates the endless fields of grass, the forest of trees surrounding us as if waking from a long slumber.

Our little house, our source of great pride. Our family.

This is my dream and wish

Away from the chaos of society of ignorant men who demand much of people, too much.

Tucked safely away by shaded trees and soft grass.

Warm sun and fresh air, this life all around us isn't controlled.

It's to be enjoyed.

Here with you, this house

This home.

Her Dark Opposite

You are soft and smooth,

And I much too hard and rough.

You are the water that cools,

Washing all pain, easing the soul.

I am the fire that burns all, consuming everything, raging inferno.

Like an angel of light,

You ascend all the love, lift others up.

Like Lucifer's demon,

I born of the dark shade within people's hearts,

Serve only to bring others down.

Sworn enemies, absolute opposites

Like Sun and Moon

Fire and Ice.

Yet steadfast lovers

Why?

Oh angel, are you the answer?

My salvation?

The answer to finding balance, can I find solace in you?

While I seek the answers to quell the hate and greed of my heart.

Yearning Inferno

Loving you was the easiest thing to do.

The hardest part?

Being away, even for a second.

My addiction off our love runs deep.

One could say it even started the moment our eyes met.

Suddenly, like a spark to a flame;

The inferno of emotions inside me threatens to overtake my consciousness.

And I am forced back into reality

With a blink, I continue writing notes

With your piercing gaze upon me.

I lust to match sight with sight,

Emotion with emotion

Intimacy and Intimacy.

Reality of Self – Awareness

Self-awareness is a double – edged sword.

The weight of knowledge,

The very essence of truth is truly a heavy burden to hold.

Knowledge is power just as much as it is pain.

We all have expiration dates,

This terrible truth is universally known.

But people choose to live in ignorance until the end.

Contemplating one's own mortality

Is a terrifying but important task.

We forget our time is limited, and sometimes this weight
freezes me in terror.

So scared I am, of losing myself…

Yet I know that's my ego speaking

Losing a sense of self,

Fear of the unknown,

Of oblivion.

These feelings we all must come to terms with.

As I grapple with this burden day by day,

I gain solace in your company,

Your presence eases the uncomfortable truth.

Because whether we choose to see it or not.

Facts and universal truths

Permeate all aspects of reality.

Ultimate Reasons

Let me tell you why you are amazing!

To this day, your acts of selflessness surprise me.

Not because it is hard for you,

Alas it is with great ease

That you care for others.

Never have I been blessed with such a kind hearted woman.

You are amazing because your love knows no bounds.

Even when hurt, your love for me never wavers.

You are amazing for the strength you give me.

Your presence revitalizes.

Two Fireflies

The best part of lying down for bed is when I can lay down beside you.

Rest is truly the best with your soft gaze upon my brow.

Let these covers hide us from the world.

For this moment with you, cherishing your silent and reassuring presence.

Like fireflies to a light source, I huddle toward your warm and soft glow.

Let this moment last forever.

My Every First

You are the only woman for me

Your touch is the only touch I need

The only woman I've made love to…

Isn't that romantic?

To be able to experience new things firsthand from now on
till my dying day with you

To me, experiences and memories are valued

And to be able to share them with you?

Heaven on Earth

Grateful Fate

Whatever makes us human I can surely find that in you.

All the good qualities you possess were not lost on my eyes.

I am so grateful for the chance of falling in love with such a
wonderfully unique person.

I am so grateful, for one kiss is all it took to seal my fate,
intertwined like never before.

Now I walk this path by your side.

There is no power greater than your love,

Like the very air I breathe,

It is a necessity for life.

For that, I am grateful.

Deeply, Infinitely, Completely

My Dear; because of you **I** finally know how **LOVE** adds a little pizazz to the ordinary.

Every day spend together is extraordinary.

Every memory shared with **YOU** is extraordinary.

From your smile to your laugh, to those beautiful hazel eyes, the window through which I gaze knowing ill have a chance to peer **DEEPLY** into you and see that unquenchable, irresistible soul that resonates to something deep within my very being, calling out to its other half.

I now know why people say we must shoot for the stars. What else must they mean than to find out lovers? For you my love, shine brightly. Why must I look up to marvel at the immensity of it all, when I can look down into your eyes and see stars upon scattered stars going on **INFINITELY** and forever.

You my darling are just so full of life, and love, **AND** happiness, it's quite infectious. In this world where life can be cruel and cold, dark and miserly,, you are the light that guides me and eases my pain **COMLETELY**; making me forget why I ever doubted this world to be a truly beautiful and worthwhile place to live in.

MY love for you is too much for this physical body to contain, you and I are one and the same person. Loving you is a gamble for I know if I ever lost you, I'd never be the same, whole person that was born the day I met you. You my **DEAR** are a gamble I'd gladly take, even if the death of that person is imminent because in this life, our forever is in the moments where we embrace, when our eyes meet and our hands touch.

Expressing my feelings for you is astronomically impossible, for there can be no words to show exactly how I feel. Just know my lover, my soul mate, my everything; this is what I mean when I say those three words…

I Love You.

My World

My world was pain. Dark skies and rough seas. Such a big, cold, scary place. Never ending was my world before you. Before that blessing, before I met you, my world was numb. Numb to the people, numb to even myself. Yet I have lived not a day wasted since the day I met you. My world is in a grasp of your tender hand. My world is in your loving gaze. My world is truly small, yet in her eyes I see entire galaxies. Your eyes my dear, hold more stars than a clear night sky. Your body is the goblet that holds what I thirst for. Like soothing water, your soul eases my parched heart. You my darling, my world. Your love washes over my aches and pains, nothing else matters. Years from now I hope my word becomes a little bigger. A small, fragile hand to hold for you and me both… but for now, the only heaven on Earth is you. The only world I know is you.

You are my world.

What is Love?

What is love, but lack of air in your presence?

To feel liberated,

To be loved,

To possess an unquenchable thirst.

If hands, feet, eyes, ears, arms and legs,

Have pairs why shouldn't hearts?

Mine is with yours,

Just as yours is with mine.

Does anything else matter?

We are doomed to die alone.

Your name will be the last words I speak.

Your essence embedded in my soul,

My distinguishing mark.

Our only worthy audience?

The stars above.

Beauty unmatched by any but nature

To lay eyes upon you and heaven,

Is there a difference?

Broken

She came from a broken home.

Her only wish was to be whole again.

Pieces of You

I saw you

I saw you 8 years ago.

But never did I think about where this would go.

Meeting you in that classroom was destined by the universe

Who works in mysterious ways.

Ways that lay claim to our hearts,

Eyes, lips, and hands that are full of touch

Such rights fluidly done

8 years later and my heart is in pieces

Not of sadness, but of eternal love

Each piece of my heart,

Infatuated with each piece of you

Be it perfection or imperfection

That's ok

Because each piece of my heart,

Like different pieces of woodchips,

Grasps each piece of you.

www.ingramcontent.com/pod-product-compliance
Lightning Source LLC
Chambersburg PA
CBHW020515160726
47991CB00007B/2963